I0556944

get rad.

THE RADVOCATE

VOL II, NO 13

MATT E. LEWIS
EDITOR

ANTHONY MUNI JR
BRIAN KRANS
KARLA AMADOR
EDITORIAL ASSISTANTS

KEITH McCLEARY
DESIGN & LAYOUTS

JESSE WILLIAMSON
WEB DEVELOPER

SEAN ANDRESS
COVER ILLUSTRATION

JUSTIN HUDNALL
EXECUTIVE DIRECTOR

Copyright © 2015, SSWA Press. All rights reserved.

ISBN-10: 0988368676
ISBN-13: 978-0-9883686-7-5

So Say We All (SSWA) is a San Diego-based 501c3 non-profit organization that provides arts education to populations without access, and supports local artists through showcase opportunities and peer-to-peer counseling.

www.sosayweallonline.com
www.theradvocateisamagazine.com

CONTENTS

INTERVIEW

FICTION

NONFICTION

A Mission Statement

Before I started *The Radvocate*, I had heard of zines before—my older brother had copies of *Cometbus* and *Automatic* that I would steal from his room when he wasn't home—and I knew that the style of DIY existed. I knew that the photocopied, crudely formatted, and don't-give-a-fuck style of writing was something that could exist in a publication. But for a kid from the suburbs, even that seemed like it was still just another component of a world I would never know. To actually take it upon oneself to make something like that, even with the most rudimentary of tools, seemed laughable. I suppose I had been conditioned that way. The idea of creating media seemed counter-intuitive, foreign, primitive—even dangerous.

In 2011, I attended a zine workshop lead by Jim Ruland, Todd Taylor, and Mike Faloon. It was at this workshop that I would learn a brief history of zines, the incredible variety of them, and their accessibility, which is revolutionary in its simplicity. Even in an age when print was 'dead', it helped me believe that I could still create something worthwhile. In my opinion, the internet didn't cut it. My belief was anchored in the idea that everyone deserves a chance to exhibit their art, poetry & writing in a print medium. That very same month, I cut up, pasted, and photocopied the first copies of *The Radvocate*. It contained a strange mélange of road fiction, incongruous fonts, rants about ego, and music critiques. In short, it was a mess. But it was a start.

It's serendipitous that other than the three leaders of the workshop, the only attendee I kept in touch with afterward was Justin Hudnall. Justin is the executive producer of So Say We All, a literary arts non-profit based in San Diego. It was through this initial meeting that I got involved with them, and discovered a community of like-minded people: writers, actors, comedians, and others who came together to create powerful public performances.

More than that, it created a space for me that I hadn't even had in college. For the first time, I had friends that not only shared my sensibilities, but my hopes, interests, and dreams. Five years later, I'm still volunteering with them, helping put on shows that connect the local community through storytelling.

In *The Radvocate*'s short lifespan, I have had the opportunity to share the work of some amazingly talented people. It opened me up to whole new worlds, things I had never considered, and hopefully gave the people who read it something to think about and enjoy. There were highs and lows, creative peaks and valleys, opportunities to experiment. But in that form, *The Radvocate* went as far as it could go. It needed space to expand, to grow, and become something more. This was something that one person couldn't provide. But then something amazing happened. So Say We All, the very same organization who had given me so much already, stepped up to the challenge. They said they believed in *The Radvocate*, what it stands for, and what it can do for the community at large. For that, I owe them my deepest gratitude, and I'm excited to explore the potential of what we can accomplish together.

To mark this, I wanted to re-affirm what our mission statement has been since the beginning: to provide a platform for people to share their art, writing, and poetry with the world. This has always been our goal, and will continue to be for as long as The Radvocate exists.

This is our thirteenth issue, but in many ways, it is another beginning. Together with So Say We All, I know that *The Radvocate* can and will grow to a level that would previously have been unthinkable. The ability to reach so many more people, to do so much more for the community, is now within our grasp. Whether you have followed us from the beginning or are just being introduced to us now, I'm excited for you. I'm excited to share fantastic new work with you from people you may not have heard of. I'm excited for you to read something that makes you think, something you wouldn't find in other publications. I'm excited for you to feel that same spark that I felt five years ago when I first created a low-budget zine and finally started to feel the things I had been searching for all my life. But most of all, I'm excited to continue to share these things with you in the years to come. And maybe inspire a few of you along the way.

Stay rad,
Matt E. Lewis
Editor-in-Chief

March 21st, 2015

ALLISON WHITTENBERG
THE QUICKENING

Because I believe in perfection
I believe in abortion
Babies are asymmetrical
They/she/he/it squander
The silken grammar of routine
But, a fetus can be edited
Its absence assures a lacy indefectibility
In the vacuum, I can breathe
It's not right
It's not the right time
I don't want to hunker down in Staten Island
Or be on bed rest
Or buy big clothes
Or rush to alter with a gown and a groom and a promise
With rice raining on me
                                    like fallout.
I don't want to be folk like my mother was folk.
Children growing out of her hairdo.
Dull eyes and unpainted nails.
Waking on the hour to feed. Feeding. Always feeding the hungry.
The weeping.
Little ones pursuing happiness.
Little ones rob happiness.
Fuzzy fussy responsibilities piling like landfills
On and on and on, like a heartbeat.

WAIT FOR RAIN

They'd have to save all the whales before they get to prisoner's rights. Still, to protect the unborn I'm cuffed in front transported on a state bus.

Will the maternity ward be pastel blue or pastel pink? It's institutional white. I'm no angel. They are no monsters. They speak in a hush.

Going under, reminds me of the high life. Like a slap, his cry kills my buzz. We bond for two years, then he's off to his sentence.

The name I gave him won't stay.

He won't remember my scent.

He doesn't have my eyes.

But maybe one day if he's not shipped too far on a side street glazed with rain. I'll pass a stranger who won't be.

THE BLACK WRITER

cold black words
corrupt the pale
virginity of paper
changing innocence
dark transforms it from
Eden, with tiny letters
that mean something,
with quick hands, you
peck the nothingness
because you are inclined to tell
the world what's on your mind
ruining the blank chastity of
empty whiteness

CROSSOVER FLIRTING

Imagine your finance's hand up my thigh,
Him telling me I looked like a Black Julia Roberts
So innocent, so hot
Something about my narrow face
My steel belted radial lips...
All right
I liked it
This being fed.
Enormous is my head
that your boyfriend's grossly blatant come ons
Hit me with fuzzy caterpillar harmlessness,
Of course, I know this ruins the echelon of things
I interfere with your zip-locked dreams of marriage
Normalcy
A house in Linden Hills
He said we were the same:
Skinny and grinny
Till then I had no idea that Hollywood's
Highest paid actress
Looked like a white version of me.

BRANDON MARLON

Hope

It is that minimal sustenance
growing wild in the clefts of rocks,
encouraging survival despite all,
a guardrail keeping us from the gorge.
Fused with confidence it becomes faith,
a trusting and wizened belief,
like a cliff-side fortress overhanging a chasm,
sheltering those reverential and humble.
Even alone it remains a unique phenomenon
full of rare meaning and power,
without which we are lost,
overwhelmed then overcome.
Yet with its seed we somehow endure,
buoyed upon the sea of our troubles,
nourished by its defiant flare,
knowing it as the handsel of success.

KIIK A.K.

A TRUMPET

The only reason you find this funny
Is you were expecting poetry
And not this other thing
About when this lamb farted
Usually when you are walking beside a lamb
That's farting you pretend not to hear it
We call that being polite
To the friend trying to teach you about lambs
You do not want to say astonished
I think your lamb is doing farts right now
Most people have heard lambs farting
But not many write poems because of it
Most people forget
But I won't forget you, little lamb
Little lamb of painful, crampy gas
And a wee mist of diarrhea
Every time I spell diarrhea I have to look it up
I always think there should be two h's
I am being careful!
Choosing just the right words
The fart was really loud!
Somehow you expected it would get muffled
Under all that wool
Like a pillow placed over the face of a loved one
But there is that lamb butthole
Raised like a little gray trumpet
Without so much wool around it
To say hush little lamb fart
A lot of people think they can get up here
And do what I do
And they're right
But who asks for this embarrassment
No one gives you cash money for that

Someone might give you money for the lamb
To cook and carry out the lamb
To sew the lamb into a purse or mask
But no one will pay for what is brief
And animal as exhalation
Though it smelled of yarrow, white sage
And a wafer of volcanic ash
And when you strangled it
It sounded something like music

ONLY VULTURES

I want you to think I am sensitive and
Not only a asshole most of the time

I cry about things sometimes
I cry so much when a dolphin is murdered

I cry about happy things too
Susan Boyle sings really good

I think what a magnificent noise
Coming from that disheveled woman's face

Think what's possible if the singer
Is actually more hotter

That is the definition of a angel
When a woman stuns you twice

First by being attractive
And then by having another quality

She's a doctor
Or says funny things

She didn't hear from anywhere else
She thought them with her actual mind

Stunning women are life's great miracles
Dolphins are number two followed by magicians

Disheveled women have their role too
But they don't exactly make me doubt

A cruel random nucleus is swallowing
Our universe from its own fucking asshole

Is there God or only vultures
Waddling with their pincers out?

I don't think I'm perfect
I go to the gym a perfect amount

But I'm still probably only a 8 or a 9
That's for white women

Asian woman standards I get somewhat better
But could you ever truly call a Asian trustworthy?

I am changing my mind on this all the time
I know I could never marry or be driven by a Asian

But could I ever actually value what a Asian thinks
Of my existence moving around on its muscles

You shouldn't think all I do is go to the gym and get strong
I am no vampire to avoid looking at my reflection

I like to laugh and look out at the stars
What do you think is out there?

I do think sometime in our lifetime
I will have to fight an alien

Do you think he will be all slimy?
I will have to fight him and maybe I'll die

I hope I die deflecting his slime to save you
I hope I cook down beside you

As I sit up my face somehow still fastened to the gravel
It sputters back it is a rash upon the rock

My muscles flare underwater
My horns fill with tears

I hope I hear you say I am still worth recovering

PULLED DOWN THE STAIRS, DRAGGED THROUGH THE LAWN

I would like for you to try and kill me
I would like for you to try and strangle me in the shower
I would like if you had no hair when you strangled me
It is not that I am upset by hair
It is that I know you are not the type to give away your DNA
    casually
I want you to take killing seriously
I want you to be naked when you try and kill me
Because you remember how liberal I am with DNA
You will not like it to muck up your dress
You will want to easily spray the DNA
From your apparently prepubescent body
You are a fan of convenience and the godliness
Of a shaved woman beneath running water
I would like for you to fail
I do not want to die just as I am getting the exact thing
I've always wanted
I would like to pass out and for you to think I expired
I would like you to lean in real close near my face with a feather
But for the vane to be too dampened to detect breathing
I would like for you to slap me a little
And pinch the tip of my cock between your fingernails
I would like you to decide you will drag me
Into the woods in my shower curtain
I would like to be wrapped up like a leftover in my curtain
And pulled down the stairs, through the kitchen
I would like for you to be sweating
And complaining about how heavy I am
I would like you to get embarrassed when you are caught
By police when dragging me through the lawn
I would like you to say it isn't what it looks like

And we are just playing a game
I would like to see you several times in court over the coming years
I would like for you to be wearing an unflattering prison jumpsuit
And for your mane to be growing in thickly
I would like for you to be forced to talk about me
About how you wrapped me in a curtain and tested my cock
I want you to say you are sorry
Even though you are assuredly less than sorry
I want you to dream of me
When trying to achieve a blackness of your mind
My bright body at the ends of your arms

PATRICK MAYUYU

MAYBE

Maybe it was gray rainy days.

Unplanned trips to Denny's after another canceled rehearsal.

I wear American Eagle too
smile
with a shoulder shrug

I didn't want to go home that night.

any night

car rides
and
you
were right beside me

The warmest shoulder

Tense

So
a little rub
between fast friends

Hands compact and stocky
the instant joy
at the sound
your voice;
Abuelita's Hot Chocolate
soft,
polite
with spice
a new sweetness I'd never tasted

My Secret
Santa
Mexican teddy bear
who loved glitter puff paint
made sure I had my own
stocking for Christmas

Found each other's smiles
across the floor

How you drove all those miles
just to dance
with us
in the frozen air of an abandoned electronics warehouse

The best place to hear your laughter echo
as we played

Maybe
it was the way the group of us
took care of
one
another

Trust that you won't drop what you just tossed in the air

Catch

I got your back

How you touched his
when I found the two of you
lying
on the floor

In the morning

Not really naked

I smiled for your happiness

Though it was abrupt
and he was still so young

A grasp I missed while in play.

Maybe we're all reaching for gold medals.

Maybe it was the way
I always wanted to hug you

The way I would deflate the heart of my practice pillow

The way we all need to be embraced

Tight

The night in the RV back from NorCal
when he was away

A game of Truth or Dare

and
we were both
a little lonely

Could not fall asleep

Maybe
there was no way for us to see
the graveled terrain ahead

So maybe
I wanted you

to leave your hand there
slithering bronzed serpent

along an undiscovered branch
a jar of a thousand trapped
synchronous fireflies
dying to burst through
mason glass

See July's gunpowder ignite in my veins

Am I radiating heat?

Was he
going to complete me?

This unplanned trip
The humid bliss
when I didn't go home

The summer I wanted to scorch my tongue
in a new sweetness I'd never tasted

(while he was away)

Praying you would leave your door ajar

Waiting to ask
if you needed a limb to swing from
something to hold on to

Tight

In a pitch black room
waiting

wanting

to breathe in the pink baby lotion
fresh out of the shower
scent
of you

Hoping you would make
your move

Knowing both of us were
a little lost

finding
each other
underneath
hands
compact and stocky

The thick throbbing
pulse
in between

I WANTED YOU THERE

making sure I was warm

(on his side of the bed)

Whisper what you would say
(to him)
in the nape of my neck

Your fingers melting my skin
the close encounter
of a touch

(forbidden)

Trying not to make a sound

As I heard you coming
as you let me have a taste
each night

26 | PATRICK MAYUYU

A little less
clothing

Pressing my body into comfort

Longing
for the length and weight
of you

(Don't mention his name)

Do you like it this way?

Maybe it was when you asked,

"Do you wanna watch a porno?"
"What?"
"...you know, get in the mood..."
"Um...no...it's ok."

warmer
warmer

Blueprint tips running smooth
over
already in the mood
uncharted
muscle

and

I've always wanted
to feel this sexy

and...

"I've always found yooouu...exotic."
"...thanks?...'exotic?'..."
"Yeah."

"Oh......
I love you."

colder
colder

and

I meant what I said
but
maybe you don't say that kind of thing
when you're
the other man
attempting to fit the mold that was made
on the other side of the bed

for
him

Another trip to Shasta Lake
the kind of stroll one takes to get their feet
wet
Maybe I was swimming too many laps
Maybe I was sinking a little too deep

Took pleasure in stroking him
naked
Learning what he was made of

Exploring his map
with my lips
his neck
his chest
his inner thighs

But he would never let me look
into his eyes

Wouldn't touch his mouth to mine

The night I was willing
to drink
every drop of his summer dark
he resisted
gave back my shirt
Turned the car around
to go home

Wash the sheets and make the bed

Maybe it was when

I cried
naive child in his arms
when
I realized I could never

I would never

I should never

have ALL of him

I am the definition of a thief caught stranded
Stained glass window crasher
Letting the holy water
evaporate
Grabbing all the horns
leaving
nothing
Graceless dancer

The worst magician you've ever seen

And maybe I can't stand
dirty mirrors
around friends who've been through this
So I steel wool scour the spots away

until
I am done
loathing my own reflection

And no one should feel sorry for a person who steals

If I could put the jar of fireflies back
on the shelf

I would

Wrap my lips
around reasoning
rather than consume
a few sweet, salty nights

Maybe if I stopped
you

Maybe if we hadn't met
Maybe if you didn't trust
Maybe summertime will always slap
me
selfish and unclean

Maybe I am unclean

Maybe I am finished
silently swallowing
and
maybe you are finally hearing me exhale

Maybe this is what ten years of sickness sounds like

A heated sigh out onto open field
means maybe
we'll take different roads
means maybe
you'll never want to see me again

I'm sorry.

Maybe
we can still be friends

Maybe.

GRANT MASON

I HAVE MY ASSESSMENT

for the United States Postal Office
in two hours.
they probably won't hire me
because of my lengthy arrest record,
detailing a history of violence and drunkenness,
but I need a job to fuel my new ideas of peace
and art
and, of course,
drunkenness.

I will drive down there in my 26 year old pick up
and put a cigarette out on the steering wheel,
wearing my paint stained jeans and burned up flannel
and walk in there and lie my way through questions of character
and hopefully get my own route
so I can drive around all day
writing poems
and delivering mail.

I'll get my own place,
a safe place,
where I can do whatever I want
after work
and count the bloody seconds of damnation
and listen for the harp string time-clocks of angels making
demands on the flower between her legs.

AND WHO SAID LITERATURE IS USELESS?

I sit here on two boxes of books
because I broke my chair.
Baudelaire, Tolstoy, Faulkner
stacked up, a tower for my ass.
Flaubert, Gide, Balzac
my bird perch as I get ready to fly
with these words I'm typing.
Dostoevsky, Whitman, Huysman
thousands of underappreciated pages in the technology age
as my little brother watches Star Trek and zombie movies for six
   hours a day
and everyone you see is on their cell phone
and the internet is the most comprehensive and accessible place of
knowledge ever known and we look at videos of porn and cats and
post pictures of our tits online and hope somebody will like our
facebook comment.
Wilde, Poe, Tennyson,
just
a tower
for my
ass.

MEG TUITE

THE BEATING LIGHT
OF AN UNDEFINED HOUR

She felt enchanted, life was an uncomplicated auction,
until a visitor saw all her luck stampeding out the door.
The rusted horseshoes she'd found in the backyard
were hung upside down. She began to slouch again,
worried she was impossible to climb. Calendars
impregnated her with white blank dates heavy
with expectation, strained by frantic engagements
she made up and penciled in. Weight of things not done
blew the gust of her into an artifact, deep cleavage
rooted her eyebrows in chronic disappointment
as her hands grew older ghosts who opened and closed
                the past like Venetian blinds.

I AM WALKING BESIDE ME

A day appears to happen cause weather is reported
and some man finds a conscience while a grocery list
blinks on the counter in capital letters no cheese no
bread sit on shelves wondering what kind of cough
magnifies the need for another afternoon on the couch
when things have generated movement though not from
inside through the lick of evening a father is absent as a
match cannot find its candle and a cemetery caws the
sound of wind chimes while the warm sound of a mother
reading stories recognizes its own past.

KNOWN SNARES OF
MESMERIC CURRENTS

Skies are roiling pink and I'm starving rooms with
the absence of you and where is nowhere that used
to hollow out the eruptive hours of indecisive head
lights gouging track marks of someone else's existence
on sullen windows painted shut and migraines dulled
by bathroom mirrors still curled around the breath of
powdered speech where laced up urgency is as close as
a woman's lipstick fat as the shaded tip of some storm
winded clothes battling the strain of dust devils driven
by the soporific fossil of unrecorded gray wishes dazed
in placid rivers crying for some kid to sweep under
waves and grasp some shiny history while inside white
spiral tiles are counted sitting on a toilet dismissed and
prophetic memories passed over waiting to be ripped
from a waiter's pad squeezed between two frightful
human tragedies of starched silence uncovered and
         strewn from wreckage of need.

MASON GREEN-RICHARDS

SLEEPER

I lay myself down,
butt first, then I spread my legs out.
The feeling of the warm silky sheets,
soothing my goosebumped hairy legs.
As I turn to my side, I place a white pillow between my legs
gaining comfort.
Closing my eyes, the daily thoughts begin to cloud my mind,
like a thunderstorm rolling into a small valley.
First, the bad thoughts come in.
"Does she like me?"
"I need to get an A on my math test."
The thoughts come in for hours,
and hours until they begin to dissipate.
I begin to not care about the girls, or the tests.
As it seems like all is peaceful, a small buzzer sound begins to
sound.
It's the sound of a new day.

PARKER TETTLETON

WHERE DO YOU GET YOUR AMINO ACIDS?

The first sentence hits pause twice, checks the internet connection—the blinks are the indecisions, the incisions, the conversions, the conversations, the hands holding a body: some format of devotion. I believe in the prayer of silence, of not asking would I exist at any other time. My feet are crossed, my clothes are clean, my submissions notebook has my full name & phone number on the inside of the cover, inscribed by my first girlfriend, who shared the losing of our virginity. It's Wednesday, I've cried twice, & I'm so very, very—.

ONE I CAN LIVE OFF

It's the day before what I don't consider to be a holiday. You don't
want to come, & you don't, to class. I leave our place five minutes
before the green line arrives at the convention center. On the way,
I tell someone who speaks *I'm in a hurry.* Fucking used to feel better than sleeping. I make the train & write through an hour & fifty
minutes of developmental psychology. I tell no one, on the way
back, plans for tomorrow.

Free Admission

We meet at the largest game store in America. After a while, we leave it. The three of us walk down a bridge & two kiss—it's a platonic book cover. A museum ahead isn't far behind. The need for a need is necessary & over. We're going to, we will, be we're going, we will.

M()

I look up the date because it is one. The second sentence is in a wood—no finish. We make up cities from pour to last. A blink is just fucking around. Do you know how you want it to be? I do. No one cares more about caring.

ZACHARY SCOTT HAMILTON

WILD

Pregnant on booze, I walk into you,
buzzing leg electrics,
frames like a fork and
image in spoons.
There I am, plastic.
Physical and demon,
dumping salt over both shoulders as we walk.
It's painted film and dream. A layer of a man,
dead, in history,
displayed
in the musty museum.
A photograph
an old man
and it's over and over
in those books too boring to read –
through windows, I
saw men in a moment, planned, altered, arranged, beautiful men.

Taking out
cypress
and eyes
to maps.

**

As a stuffed bird,
sound blends through a
spine
and it blends into blood and
whiskey
sugar,
and my thin bones
and the chalk board writes alone in one corner.

***

Celebrate a
partaking in madness while feasting on
rhythms,
on the confusion of feasting.
Liars
decided in fear, to
feast on the cold glare of lights,
on the ladies jade
and the blind eyes.
We stagger to darkness
tonight, to run far.
At the train tracks
smoking.

***

Twist beyond now
trying too hard,
to place your fingers
into a laugh.

Tease neck and cry neck,
lovely here
forgive.

Crazed,
broken, stolen, stealing and broke. Inside this need
toss up. Grimace, destroyed face in spin wheel laying above me.
Caught by the spider
waste, poison, trapped between physical self.
Call me, they stabbed my rat to the table. Release it.
Origin. Promise.
Chaos, love.
To remain in challenged attention. This truth.
Trust me.

He sailed into a land known as the Isidore
window, only explained by numbers

Exposed to the idiosyncrasies of
Quinn, who brought such imbecile conclusions.
Blending with frequent bursts of light, he rose to the caverns
into a plateau of his lonely existence, and the rain answered
questions, that he lost in a wandering night

Sheets of plastic allowed lightning into the center of his dwelling.
Great fire inside.

Night owls go out to fly away
the flux of accord
listen for the sound

it had been haunting, this daily routine, forgiving him,
for those mundane, curled bottles of cabernet and pinot noir,
      questioning
the re-collections of Quinn. Encrypted poems were then found
      neatly folded
in his secret pocket.

To down another swill of Cabernet.
The night young
wondering about this number ten, only for old insane
house could he ever imagine beauty like friends
Trinity in the garden, abandoned house, flooded with green algae,
the river half a mile down, snakes and old toys under the wake, in
the garden.

Trinity grows maple trees and ancient flowers, storing them in
a lockable cage –
shadows shift all over the surface
programmed to understand, through language
nowhere –
the place you end up.

CLAY NORVELL

A CONVERSATION WITH
HENRY ROLLINS

I don't remember how I came upon the book, but after reading
Eye Scream *by Henry Rollins, I decided I wanted to write.*

*I was a fourteen year old kid immersed in punk rock, skateboard-
ing, and the oppressive environment of the public school system,
which is to say I was rebellious, yet easily impressionable. Ideals
and ideas that once made so much sense to me are now laughable
rants written by people who found interesting ways to say nothing more than they were tired of being ignored or angry. That's
not to say* Eye Scream *is like that at all – far from it, actually.
What that book told me was that I wasn't alone when it came to
thinking dark things, and that it was ok to be different.*

*So when I had a chance to meet Henry Rollins in 2008, I made a
copy of my own forty page manifesto, which I have to admit was
meant to be a tribute, but could easily be considered a rip off of
his style.*

*In the years since, Henry and I have stayed in touch sporadical-
ly, and when I forgot to write to him on his birthday last year, I
finally sent him a message and asked if he would be interested in
answering a few questions I had...and here's the result.*

CN: Like you, I'm a voracious reader. While I continue to buy
printed books, I also recently jumped on the Kindle bandwagon
and the experience isn't as harrowing as I once believed it might
be. Have you purchased or used an E-reader device, or are you
sticking to printed books?

HR: I had a couple of e-books but it wasn't all that good for me.
Now I have several but it's for a television show I am working on.

All of us making the show have the same account access so we can all check numerous books for reference. It's handy but I would rather have a real book to read. The books I read these days, I tend to mark up a lot and it's just easier to deal with them as real things, not on a battery operated device.

CN: On *Talk is Cheap Volume 1* (2000), you were celebrating your fortieth birthday, saying that it wasn't any kind of a milestone. You went on to say [paraphrased] that, "getting a new tattoo at fifty was badass." You're known for your array of tattoos already, but did you get a new tattoo at fifty, or do you have plans to do get any new ones?

HR: I don't plan on it. I am not interested in doing anything more to my exterior. I would rather just stay in shape and see what my mind can do. If someone wants to get something done on them at a later age, I think they should. For me, at this point, I am only interested in what I can do and what I can understand.

CN: One of my favorite quotes of yours is "Rage keeps the blood thin." Are there any new issues in the world now that are bringing out the rage?

HR: I am saddened and angered by the way so many people have thrown themselves in with those who do them harm. In America, money goes to the top and stays. There is no trickling down, there is no benevolent master who feeds the teeming masses below with the crumbs that fall from his bountiful table. It's amazing how many Americans fell for it. If you have spent any meaningful time on the streets, you would have seen what's happening coming right at the start. I saw it in the summer of 1984 and started planning how to survive and prosper. I was right about everything and my plans were very helpful. I am mad that America is back to where, or at least heading towards, where it was before 1865. There are a few rich and a lot of poor. I guess this is what these people wanted. Doesn't look like it's working out too well for them. A rage for living is a good thing. I am curious and angry, so every day is a challenge and an adventure. Might not be for everyone but it's good for me.

CN: You've also said before that you "don't know how to sing," which I personally don't believe for an instant, but opinions aside, it's an undeniable fact that you aren't someone who wastes time or effort for any reason, so why would you continue to do it for 30+ years if you didn't believe you could do it?

HR: Just because I can't sing doesn't mean I can't play with a band and get a point across. I knew I could do it, but also knew it was always going to be on the outskirts of interest. Once you are okay with that, then you can get to work and get things done.

CN: The output of books, CDs, and music has steadily declined over the past few years, aside from the recent release of *Before the Chop*...what is 2.13.61 doing these days?

HR: I don't do music anymore, so there's no records. I used to do talking records but since they get posted online and downloaded for free, I don't see the point. I do a lot of writing, the weekly radio show, voice over work, television and film. So, I am actually busier than ever but the output is different. The publishing company works on my stuff mainly. My new book *A Grim Detail* is at the printer right now.

CN: Punk music was once an outlet for pent-up aggression. Now there are "punk" bands that write happy songs. Can these two things coexist, or are these new bands doing it wrong?

HR: Of course they can. You listen to what you want and skip the rest. There is no such thing as wrong music. What would you say to a band working away in a garage, "Sorry, you'll have to stop. Your music is wrong. What did you guys call yourselves? The Clash? What a stupid name. Alright, turn it all off and pack up." As soon as you throw out all the classifications and just get on with checking out the music you like, the better off you'll be I think.

CN: Rollins Band hasn't been active since 2006. Will you go on the road in the year 2035, like Iggy did with The Stooges after a twenty-nine year hiatus?

HR: I don't think so. I am not interested in the past in that way. Life is too short for repeats.

CN: Greg Ginn recently blew a gasket and started up a string of frivolous litigation against anyone associated with Black Flag. Did it come as a surprise to you that he would make you a target after 26 years?

HR: I was surprised that he didn't seek better legal advice. It didn't go at all well for him.

CN: Have you heard the new Black Flag album, and if so, do you have any thoughts on it? (Side note, a friend of mine who I'm sure you know, Stephen Egerton, is involved with the project FLAG. They seem to be much more popular than any of Greg's undertakings have ever been. Have you heard any of their stuff?)

HR: I did hear a couple of songs. I can't say it moved me in any way. I think to occupy battlefields of the past and think you're fighting is lame. If you have ever seen a war reenactment, that's what these bands are doing. It is for them to do but it is what it is.

CN: You haven't had children yet, but it's not too late. Who is going to be the voice of reason for the next generation if there isn't a Rollins progeny?

HR: I think the next generation will do just fine without a trace of my DNA. There are enough people in the world.

CN: One of the best Black Flag songs that you did vocals for, in my opinion, was "My War." In 2006, when you re-recorded it for the *Rise Above* CD, you came full circle and made it YOUR song. Your voice and emotion in that recording is downright devastating (in the best way possible). I still get chills listening to it. After twenty plus years, do you still feel all the anger that most of the Black Flag catalog stood for?

HR: I do. It's a strange thing being mad all the time but that's basically how I am.

NEIL P. McDEVITT

THE MOLES

Mike

I was hanging out at high school with my friend Mike. We had
just spent a couple of hours preparing for a debate team match
and had gone to the boy's room before leaving the building. I was
walking out ahead of Mike when I heard him behind me.

"Oh God!" he practically shouted.

I turned to see what the problem was.

He came out and said, "I just glanced my reflection in the mirror
and saw myself without realizing it was me."

I shrugged, not comprehending what he meant.

"I saw myself the way other people must see me," he said. "It
wasn't pleasant." He paused and asked, "Do you know what I
mean?"

I thought a moment and said, "Yeah, I think that I do."

The Mirror

I stood shirtless at the bathroom mirror in the apartment I shared
with Catherine. She was out of town for the weekend with friends.
On the sink I had placed a pair of toenail scissors and a styptic
pencil, the kind men use to close shaving nicks by burning them
shut. I examined my face, turning my head from side to side. I
couldn't decide which one to start with.

On the left side of my face, there were two moles, one just above
my eye and one below. On the right side there was a mole between

my right sideburn and my ear and one a little lower down. The last one was to the left of my chin.

I decided to start with the one by my ear, since it was the least obvious, in case it went wrong. I picked up the toenail scissors and held them against my skin, with the mole in between the blades. I took a deep breath. Then I slowly squeezed the scissors closed. At first the mole bulged between the small shears, then it disappeared.

I looked down at the sink, trying to find the mole, but it wasn't there. This confused me. I hadn't expected the mole to come flying off, like a thick toenail cut away will sometimes do. I figured it would drop straight down. I scanned the sink again and then the floor. I didn't want to leave a mole lying around. That would be untidy. I stood up from the floor and then I saw it.

It was lying on the sink, but it was hard to see. On my face it had been a medium brown color, but cut off, it was a pale white, nearly the same color as the porcelain. I went to press it against my forefinger and pick it up. Just then it was joined by a large red splat. I looked up in the mirror and saw a trickle of blood running down my face. I glanced down again and a second bright red drop fell a few inches from the first.

I took some toilet paper and pressed it to my face over the small wound where the mole had been. Then I picked up the styptic pencil. I pressed the pencil on the cut and rubbed it in. It burned, but only slightly.

Brian

Brian and I lived together in Brighton during college. We spent many lazy days slouching around the kitchen table, drinking coffee, smoking cigarettes, and talking about nothing much. One time we fell onto the subject of my appearance, and what was wrong with it.

"Well, I have a big nose," I said, "and that's a defect."

"Yeah," Brian said, "It is kind of wide, but what about the profile?"

I shrugged and he told me to turn my head to the side.

"Well, your nose isn't that bad in profile, but your weak chin kind of ruins that."

I'd never thought of myself as having a weak chin, but it seemed plausible enough. Then Brian leaned in closer. "What is that on your face? A mole?"

"Yeah, there are two right there," I said, pointing them out as I spoke.

"I guess that's not your good side," Brian said, and then, "turn your head the other way."

I turned my head and he said, "Oh, there's a mole there too."

I nodded.

"So I guess you don't have a good side," he said with a light laugh before adding, "Sorry man."

I shrugged it off. "No need to apologize if what you're saying is true," I said.

Brian heard my tone and winced a little. "Maybe not," he said, "but I still shouldn't have said it."

The Mirror

The bleeding stopped and I examined what was left. The entire mole was gone, flush to my face. Looking right at it, it didn't look great, a purplish white mix of dried blood and the styptic. But when I turned my head there was nothing there, unlike the mole which had stood out in profile relief. This was a real improvement. I picked up the off-white remains of the mole and dropped it in the toilet. I scanned my face looking for the next one to remove.

I switched to the left side of my face and brought the scissors up to the mole above my eye. When I sliced it off, it also fell right onto the sink, pale white. After cauterizing with the styptic pencil to stop the bleeding, I picked it up and flicked it into the toilet with the first.

I examined my face and tried to imagine what scar would remain in a couple of days. I decided it would probably be fine.

My Father

My father and I were sitting in the kitchen, my senior year of high school.

"I see you cut yourself shaving," he said.

"Yeah I did," I said. "It's annoying because there's a mole there and I can't really shave around it."

"You know, if you went to a doctor, he could get rid of that for you."

"Like how?" I said.

"Oh, they can just freeze it with liquid nitrogen and it will come right off," he explained.

This seemed implausible to me, even though my father said it with great confidence.

"You should bring that up with your doctor," he advised me further, "and get it taken care of."

I nodded my head, suggesting I would do just that. But I was seventeen and had not seen a doctor since I broke my arm in eighth grade. I didn't know the name of my health insurance provider or an appropriate doctor to see. I suppose I could have asked my father for that information, but I didn't.

The Mirror

It felt like the twenty minutes of effort had taken all day. I kept taking long breaks to stare over the scabs on the moles I'd already removed and look at the ones I still had to deal with. The first couple had had really clean lines on the edge where my skin ended and the mole began. But the last one was less distinct, and when I cut it the result wasn't as good. There was still a bump there and I almost tried to cut it a little deeper. But I didn't want to leave a hole in my face.

I saved the mole on my chin for last. It was square in the middle of my face, so whatever happened with it was going to be very obvious. I wondered if I should wait a few days to see how the others healed up before cutting it away. I looked down in the toilet at the moles I was already rid of. They were floating below the surface of the water, translucent like tiny jellyfish. I flushed them down. Then I turned back to the mirror to finish the job.

Catherine

"Can I ask you something?" Catherine said, interrupting me while I was watching the football game.

"Sure."

She sat down and looked me in the eye. "I was thinking about if we ever had kids, or, if we had a daughter," she said slowly, "well, if she had one of those things on her face. . ." Catherine trailed off making a sort of grimace.

I interrupted her. "You mean a mole?" I said, lifting my hand to my face and pressing on one with my thumb.

"Yeah, a mole," she confirmed. "Well, I'd want us to take her to a doctor right away to get it removed."

I nodded.

"I mean, I wouldn't want her to have that on her face, you know?"

I nodded again. "Yeah Catherine, that would suck. If that happens we should get it taken care of right away."

Catherine smiled at me, relieved.

Then she looked a little embarrassed. "I mean, a little girl wants to be pretty, you know, it matters more."

"Yeah, I see what you mean," I said. Then I returned my attention to the game. I didn't think there was much else to say.

The Mirror

I was finally ready to cut that last mole off my chin. I held the scissors with the arc of the blades lying down so that the tips stood a bit off of my face. For the last time that day I snipped away. But it wasn't like the other times. It was tougher and I had to press harder to cut through. And there was more blood.

I grabbed a tissue and dabbed at it, but as soon as I pulled it away, the hole filled with blood, quickly, before I could tell if I had cut off the entire mole. Even though I couldn't see very clearly, I could tell there was an edge along the high side of it that hadn't been removed.

I decided to trim that edge, before trying to stop the bleeding. I leaned forward letting the blood drip down my chin into the sink. Then I cut at the edge and spun a thick wad of toilet paper off the roll, holding it against my face, pressing hard.

I started to feel sick. The pain was bearable and I hadn't lost much blood really, just a few drops, but I was stricken with fear. I imagined a hideous scar in the middle of my face and how I would have to admit I had put it there myself. Suddenly the whole project seemed idiotic and disgusting. Who cuts moles off their own damned face with toenail scissors? I wondered what people would think and how I would explain it.

I took a deep breath and tried to settle down. I held the styptic pencil under the water to soften up the surface into a paste. Then I smeared it on, extra thick. It burned like hell. I had to do it three times before the bleeding stopped.

I slumped against the sink, worn out from the effort and the thought that I had made a terrible mistake. I went to the bedroom and lay down on my back, stretching my arms out to either side. I wanted to fall asleep, but I didn't want to turn over and peel away a scab. Catherine was very fond of the pillowcases.

Catherine

By the time Catherine returned home, my face was mostly healed. Two of the moles had come away so cleanly you could hardly tell they were ever there and even the one on my chin looked okay. Catherine walked into the living room to kiss hello but she stopped just short, taken aback.

"The moles are gone," she said.

"Yeah," I said, "I removed them."

"You removed them?" She said.

"I just felt like it."

She examined my face. "It looks better," she decided.

I nodded at her inanely, trying to gauge her reaction. I decided she was trying to be encouraging so I mustered my best smile and said, "I'm glad you think so."

ALAN SEMROW

Hydroponic Nights

Dude, we got the table in the middle, just having a good time. Freddie is all like, "This is hydroponic weed—it'll get you stoned off one hit. So you gotta be careful or you're gonna be just over your head."

Our spread here, it's lighters and pipes and bongs. Right now, Sammy's teaching Tyler how to use the purple bong, 'cuz he's a newb and he doesn't know as much as the rest of us.

One of those younger types—probably a virgin.

Between Tyler's coughing fits, Sammy asks me how it's going with Annie.

I narrow my eyes and stare into his. I see angels kissing. I say, "Who the fuck is Jennifer?"

We all burst out in a fit of laughter. It's just good times, man.

We got the Doritos in the middle. We're not quite nibbling, more like gorging. Everyone's fingers are a bright, cheesy orange. Our teeth and lips are all the same color. In the background, we got the latest Eminem rhymes playing.

Brotherhood comes before anything else, that's the one thing that I've learned in my short life. As long as you got your guys to lean on, to talk to—you should be alright. I mean, shit does happen, but as long as you just accept the fact that you got a lot of love in your life, then I suppose there's no reason for everything not to be alright.

"So," Sammy says. "How's you and Annie doing?"

I laugh so hard that a tear streams down my face. The tear feels like a crystal from a chandelier.

Freddie opens his mouth and he says, "I fucked her last Saturday. It's all good."

I shake my head at the motherfucker. Shame, shame. See, a brotherhood, that's all you got sometimes in your life.

I ask Freddie how he got all this shit and, as I do, the whole room erupts in fear and gasps. I look at Freddie and he's shaking his head in disappointment. He says, "Isn't this the shit."

Freddie stands up and walks to the cage where his pet ferret, Miley, resides. He opens the gate and reaches in for little Miley. I watch in a haze, Miley climbs up his arm and Freddie grips her long frame. He pets with the other hand. It's almost like he's snake-handling. Almost.

It's all like God has come down and given the two of them his blessing. You wish for a family in life and then you wake up one morn and it's all in front of you. Freddie, Miley, Sammy, and Tyler—all I need. My bros.

Freddie sits back down on the old, rotting couch. He looks me in the eyes and says, "You never, ever ask where a motherfucker who is providing you weed got their shit." He shakes his head at me again. I think I feel embarrassed, but I also feel a lot of things right now. Like the world is in front of me, like I could dig a hole and drive it all the way to China.

We have a moment of silence. Eminem is rapping about crude subject matter. He's amazing though. I mean, to just have this gift—this gift that he gives back. To come up with this shit on the tippy top of a moment. I wonder for a second if maybe Eminem is Jesus reborn.

We're all just staring at each other. Not one of us moves except for little Miley, who Freddie is holding onto tightly.

"Ya'll gonna crash here tonight?" Freddie asks, as if we haven't been crashing here for days. Everyone that is, but Tyler—he's new here. Sometimes, we get new folks in our crowd and they stay with us until they go and fuck one of our babes or something special like that.

We keep things up, though. We keep things going. We keep things interesting.

My ear is on all things. My sense of smell, of sight, of hearing—it's all very taut, clear. Tyler tells Freddie that he has the intention to stay here long.

Sammy says, "Now don't be fucking any of our girls though."

"I'm gay," Tyler says.

We all erupt in laughter. Freddie puts a hand around Tyler's shoulders and says, "Well, I can promise you we all won't be fucking any of your boyfriends."

I smile, thinking about that night with Freddie, under the stars—on mushrooms.

The room goes quiet again. I look Freddie in the eyes.

I hear the sirens, sirens, sirens. The music keeps playing. We all stay put. Miley squirms.

Sometimes, all you really have is your brotherhood. Not much of a job, not much of a family, not much of a love life—just your brotherhood.

As the sirens become more and more prominent, closer and closer and closer, Sammy asks, "So how's everything going with Annie?"

ROBIN WYATT DUNN

THE VENUSIAN ARTIST RESIDENCY

The yellow here is my least favorite color; it cascades over the plexiglass like piss. Quantum piss, perhaps, since the storm stretches all matter into the craziest of shapes.

Artist residencies are not unlike religious retreats; I am the Stylite, behold, atop my Venusian tower, blind as a bat and closer to God than ever . . .

Hogwash, but it sells books. It moves paintings. Puts fresh pressed records into the teeny boppers' hot little hands, and I am popular now, so popular, so goddamned popular, in my box, on Venus, like a surfer drop shipped onto a five hundred foot wave, alone in the universe and broadcast live . . .

My room is artfully arranged, comfortable. A bear rug. A fake but convincing fireplace. They wouldn't give me any video games; I am here, after all, to create.

The yellow is my least favorite; I feel ill for hours after one of the yellow-light storms.

The blue-green are beautiful, though, like ancient Neptune angry but subdued, behind glass, I'm on the Disneyland ride, 10,000 leagues and twenty atmospheric pressures under, an MFA graduate, loneliest man in the solar system . . .

\- -

In the east another one is coming; I wish I were Turner, but I am a modernist. If I were Turner I could capture its fluid beauty, storm on storm like two Mississippis meeting, the outflow fractally specific and luminous, light fomenting change and death and the cruelest of all imaginable summers, hot pink fuchsia eglantine waves ravaging brown outcropping jags, this planet is a drug I cannot seem to acclimatize to—

Of course our moods are prisoners of the weather, of course they are, but our moods were designed for terrestrial rain, not Venusian—

The result is like lacing the coffee addict's morning cup with crack; acid in the eggs.

- -

I wonder how it is being edited. Whether my pounding on the glass and my tears and my "revolutionary" turd in the middle of my room (even though I'm the one who has to smell it) made it onto the screens of the average Earthling, or whether they even use my face at all. Perhaps that's it; a queer reversal of the old Fake Apollo Moon Landing conspiracy theory; I am actually on Venus but they fake it back on Earth anyway, because it makes for better camera angles, and a more handsome face . . .

- -

When I return I will no longer be the same. True for any journey of course but for me, this one, it feels as I imagine the political prisoner might, at last released from the torture chamber . . .

- -

Yellow is the color of madness; I fear it has taken me with it. My next canvas will be a thousand yellows, and I will paint it with my face . . .

ALEX BOSWORTH

No Day at the Beach

Years ago, I took this girl to the beach. Unfortunately, as we were driving, the sky turned cloudy and by the time we got there, it had started raining. We sat in the car waiting for it to clear up, but it didn't.

So we drove around for a while, trying to think of something else to do and ended up at an aquarium. Once inside, we walked around looking at the fish, because it was an aquarium and that's pretty much all you can do there. Eventually, my date got bored and suggested we sneak into the men's room and smoke a joint.

"What?!" I said. "You've had weed this whole time? Seems like we could have skipped the whole aquarium thing. We were sitting in a car at the beach for God's sake! That's pretty much why they invented cars! And beaches, I'm pretty sure!" I checked to make sure the men's room was empty, then waved her in. We lit up a fatty in the handicapped stall and were having a pretty good time when a man came in and used the stall next to us. After he flushed, we thought we were in the clear but I guess he saw our feet under the stall.

"Hey, why are there four feet down there?" he asked.

Thinking quickly, I made an animal noise. "Ba-a-a-a-a"

"Oh." the man said. "So, you're a sheep."

"Well, I was kind of going more for a goat kind of thing."

"Ah. You're a goat then."

"That's right. I'm a goat."

"Why are you wearing shoes?"

"It was raining. Um, so how are you?"

"Pretty good. I was at the beach, but like you say, it started raining, so I decided to drop some acid and go to the aquarium."

"That's so funny! Practically the same thing happened to us!"

"What you mean 'us'?"

Once again, I had to think quickly. "I'm pregnant."

"Oh, congratulations. What are you hoping for?"

"Well, I already have a nanny, so this time I'd like a billy. Of course, I'm really just hoping for a healthy kid."

"Well, good luck." he said, preparing to leave. "Hold on, shouldn't you be in the ladies room?"

"The handicapped stall was being used in there."

"You're handicapped?"

"Yes. I have a prosthetic hoof. Guess which one."

"Hmm. Front right?"

"Interesting. Everyone guesses front right. But no, rear left."

"Well, you can't tell."

"Thanks. Wait, you think I'm the kind of goat who'd use a handicapped stall even though she's not really handicapped? How dare you?! Good day, sir!"

"I'm sorry. I didn't mean to-"

"I said good day!"

After the guy left, we decided to stand on the toilet. We were almost done with our joint when someone else came in. I could see over the top of the stall that it was the security guard. "Anyone in here?" he said. Then he flipped off the lights, stepped out and locked the door.

Assuming we were trapped for the night, we began to think of ways we could pass the time until the aquarium re-opened. I can't say I'd recommend playing charades in the pitch black in an aquarium bathroom unless you're really high. Luckily we were, so it was actually a lot of fun. After an hour, it dawned on me to try the door, which opened, having only been locked from the outside. I can only assume this is done to keep criminals from stopping off to use the facilities during burglaries. We wandered out into the aquarium to find ourselves completely alone with only the dim, blue-green light of the tanks illuminating the halls.

"It's so cool in here." my date whispered. Then she pulled off her sweater and tossed it to the floor. "Hey, are you thinking what I'm thinking?" I watched wordlessly as she began unbuttoning her shirt.

"Come on. Take off your pants. Let's do it!"

"What?" I thought. "Expose ourselves to the fish? Is that even a thing?" By the time she'd undressed and was grinding her body against mine, I'd begun to think she had something of an erotic nature in mind. After she'd removed my clothing, I laid her down on a nearby viewing bench and we went to business, as the young folks like to say.

Things were going really nicely, until I looked up to see this fish staring at us. The others were just swimming along, paying no notice, but this one sea bass just kept looking right at us with an intense gaze. I tried not to let it bother me, but then it started saying things in a really low voice.

"Yeah!" it said. "You hit that, boy! You hit that hard! Mmm!"

I continued as if I didn't hear anything, but then he started saying stuff that was really out of line. "Uh huh! That's it! You got what she's been beggin' for! You split that timber, young woodsman!"

"Okay, hold on!" I said. "Split that timber?! What the hell is that?!"

"I'm just trying to help you out!" the bass replied. "I'm on your side, man! I'm rootin' for you over here!" I tried to get back to the act, but this bass just wouldn't keep his big mouth shut. Plus, it was becoming pretty obvious he was getting off on the whole scene.

"Oh, yeah! You are working her, my man! This is so... ooh! Ugh! You really... you've got her... mmm!"

"Yo! Mr. Limpet! Keep it down, all right! You're ruining it for me!"

"No! You're ruining it for me. So just shut up and get back at it!"

"You're telling me to shut up?!"

Finally, my date grew impatient. "What's the matter?" she asked. "Am I doing something wrong?"

"No, no! You're fine." I told her. "It's just this fish with all the dirty talk. I mean, look! It's all pressed up against the glass. And all that stuff about workin' it and hittin' that."

"What? You don't like it?" she said.

"Not really, no. Why? Do you?"

"Look, just pretend we're all alone, okay? Come on! Let's split some timber!"

So I started in again and although the other two sides of this amphibious triangle were clearly popping their corks, there was something about having Charlie Tuna as a voyeur that made it a tad difficult for me to reach cloud nine. Consequently, my partner and the peeping tom cod managed to achieve simultaneous orgasm, whereas I was forced to relinquish long before any chance of sticking my own personal landing.

I guess I'm not all that romantic. I mean, I should probably look back on the experience with fondness. After all, I did smoke some good pot and make love to a woman at an aquarium. But I can't help dwelling on those awkward moments afterwards, fumbling around in the dark, trying to find my clothes. Then clumsily putting them back on. And all the while, this girl asking me why I wasn't able to finish and the fish offering to help. It was a nice enough date, I guess.

But it was no day at the beach.

RYAN HICKS

THE ALLEY MAN

Tap. Tap. Tap.

Was the sound on the window, of the house, in the neighborhood, that was supposed to be safe. Creating the first set of fingerprints on the outside of the glass. From the alley, that was dirty. Filled with garbage, and weeds, and waste, and him. Pacing up and down, back and forth, all night, while everyone rests, and sleeps, and dreams.

Tap. Tap. Tap.

Is what my little sister and I heard over the hum of the television, the glow of the nightlight, the stillness of security. Freezing our bones. Calling to attention the light, thin hairs on our soft bodies. Stunting our organs. Squeezing our guts. Pure fear, in the fortress of peace.

Tap. Tap. Tap.

We turned to see a man staring in at us. The window was high up but he filled the entire frame. Long, wiry hair. Balding on top. Dusty wrinkles scarring his cheeks and forehead. Crooked glasses over prying eyes. He was breathing heavily onto the glass, creating a mini mushroom cloud of condensation. Hot and wet. Appearing and disappearing. A fast healing wound.

Our eyes met his. For just a moment. A flash of penetration. His leering gaze, full of blood and cum and desperation and control, held us paralyzed... Then released.

The house filled with the pitter patter of our tiny feet, normally reserved for playtime, frantically running passed barely locked doors and open windows to the master bedroom where mom and dad had been jolted awake by our terrified cries bouncing through the halls and off the ceiling.

The rabid electricity of threat.

I usually took care of my sister, but as we ran from those wide open, blood shot eyes all I could think of was escape. It was the first time I was truly afraid. Our parents lied to our faces and we believed them. "Everything is ok." "It was probably just an accident." "There is nothing to worry about."

Comfort is short lived. Embrace is temporary. Damage is done.

***

This happened when I was 10 years old. We had just moved in to our upper middle class West Texas suburb. The block meeting the neighbors held was for us. To tell us what they knew, which wasn't much. The alley man had visited once before, to several houses, but only the families living on the west side of the street.

It started with the lights. Every once in a while many of the outside garage and porch lights would turn off. Not because they had burned out, because they had been unscrewed.

This was just the beginning of what began to happen every few months.

***

One woman found a chair sitting right in front of her bathroom window, next to a giant pile of cigarette butts and beer bottles.

One morning, pages of pornography papered backyards and danced in the wind around swing sets and into pools.

One night, after everyone had left bags of used clothing to be picked up for donation, he emptied them, burned holes into the chests and crotches of dresses and pants, and hung them from the trees in our front yards.

But, he'd never tried to break in or hurt anyone. Every time a neighbor would call the cops to report the behavior, the police would just say there's nothing they could do. He would have to be caught in the act, but his visits were so sporadic there was no way to know when he'd be back.

Several weeks later, dad came home late after a long day at work. As he was pulling into the driveway he came to screeching halt. Someone was standing there. Dad was so surprised he didn't even realize who it was. By the time he did it was too late to report it or try to find him.

Thud. Thud. Thud.

Shook the walls of my sister's bedroom, which was right on the other side of the alley. She thought it was me. Messing with her. Pulling a prank. But when she looked in I was still sleeping. She went slowly back into her room and it got louder. She leaned over just enough to see out into the alley, and there he was. Standing with her window's screen in one hand and a knife in the other.

Her scream woke me up. This time the fear felt familiar, like a language of learned behavior. We exploded into the hallway and into our parents' arms. Again. They had heard the pounding from the other side of the house.

He wasn't just watching anymore. All of the screens on the alley side windows were slashed. Others had experienced a similar disturbance, and this was enough to finally get the city to install big bright lights down the alley. Bars were placed on everyone's windows and for a while, he was gone.

Tap. Tap. Tap.

***

It was a couple years later. I was watching television. Laying on the same couch in the same back room where I first laid eyes on him.

Tap. Tap. Tap.

I couldn't move. My stomach turned. The sounds from the TV went mute and all I could hear was skin on glass. Heavy breathing. Heart pounding. Trembling. "Maybe it's the wind." His hand hit harder each time. Ticking like the timer on a bomb building to an explosion. Fear could only do so much to keep me from giving in to this panicked curiosity by forcing myself to look to confirm this was real. That it was really him. That he was really back.

Tap. Tap. Tap. Tap. Tap. Tap...

I finally sat up to see him. We made eye contact for one (breath) sharp inhale before he finished turning to walk away. At least, my eyes told me he walked. My brain told me he floated. He looked sicker. Less human. Thinner. Dirtier. Longer hair. Like a decomposing corpse.

This time I didn't run. I was supposed to be a man, but was reminded of my youth in my complete inability to get his twisted face out of my head. I was shaking as I woke up dad. He called a neighbor who was comforting his crying young girls. They thought the alley man was trying to get into their bedrooms.

I sat quietly in the backseat as dad drove our neighbor, armed with a baseball bat, up and down the streets looking for him. They had called the police who were also patrolling.

I thought back to the summer of our first encounter. That next morning, my sister and I, as curious as we were afraid, walked around the front of the street to the end of the alley. We looked down to see a man putting something in a dumpster. It surely wasn't the alley man, but at the time, in our young minds, it was. He was so far down the alley I couldn't even make out what I was seeing. Just a big, dark, shadowy figure. So that is what I started looking for.

But dad slammed on the breaks and our neighbor jumped out of the front seat, chasing the real alley man into the black shade of the giant trees that lined the sidewalk. We waited, ready to help, or run, or call the cops again... Until our neighbor returned, alone, out of breath, and disoriented. He said, "I know this sounds crazy, but I swear to god he just disappeared. Vanished right in front of me."

Maybe he had floated away from my window. I grabbed dad's hand. He squeezed. I let go. Be a man. Dad bent down and said, "He's gone now. Let's go home. We'll take care of it tomorrow." And again, I believed him.

Mom still credits the next block meeting as one of the most surreal things she's ever experienced. Kids weren't allowed at this one. Once sane, polite members of upper middle class suburbia were reduced to scared villagers in the wake of a witch-hunt. It was quiet before someone suggested starting a neighborhood watch. There was a gentle buzz of acceptance, until a man shouted, "Let's just kill him" which started a back and forth between bold threats and levelheaded reasoning. They eventually settled down and accepted that the police had done all they were able to do. The parents saw no other way. The plan was to buy guns, sit on the roofs in shifts until he returned, and then shoot him. Dead or alive.

Bang. Bang. Bang.

Was the sound of the gavel on the bench during the alley man's trial.

Before anyone had a chance to shoot him, he was arrested. He had established enough of a pattern and when the cops caught wind of the plan, they decided to be around more than usual.

Finally, something was done.

The trial was fairly uneventful. A man who dad worked with was on the jury. The alley man had gone to high school with a woman down the street. He was the valedictorian of their class and

70 | RYAN HICKS

apparently had a schizophrenic break in college. This mentally-ill, supposedly-medicated man lived over an hour away and was driving into town on random nights with no discernible pattern and parking at the church down the street.

As the trial ended and the alley man was escorted out of the court-room, his last words were, "You think you've won, but this isn't over."

***

Most of the charges were dropped due to lack of evidence. He was eventually released.

He never came back, but in a way, he never left.

I didn't hear about the block meeting or the trial or his past until years later. Our parents always tried to play it off, hoping each incident would be the last. My sister and I were never given up-dates unless we asked. Some sort of selective amnesia allowed us to get through our youth without being constantly terrified, but we always made sure that doors and windows were locked. We jumped whenever branches brushed the glass or if animals trashed the alley. Even now I can't sleep unless my blinds are closed.

Every childhood has a boogeyman.

Mine just happened to be real.

They told me his name.

johnnie b. baker

THE PROGRAM

I was in Los Angeles County Jail for failure to pay a speeding ticket. I had already been in for a couple days when I was transferred to Wayside, the maximum-security county jail in the hills. Keeping people moving is one way to deal with overcrowding. This was the jail for people doing real county time, those on trial, or those on their way to state prison.

I was given a mattress with the others I arrived with and placed in a large, already full cell block. Each cell in the block had dozens of triple-bunk beds, chairs and tables bolted to the floor, toilet and shower stalls and a row of payphones. There were six or so locked cells surrounding the central desk area, where the deputies were stationed.

I laid my mattress on the floor against an empty wall and sat down, keeping in mind my mantra "Don't speak unless spoken to." I noticed the make-up of the hundred some inmates I had joined, Blacks and Mexicans about split down the middle. I was the only white person. I sat against the wall, laid on my mattress, and kept to myself.

Some of the deputies came around and started handing out newspapers through the cell room bars. Something to read! But there was no way I would get one, people gathered at the bars grabbing them and I wasn't about to attempt to grab one.

Then, "Hey white boy!" I was the only one in the cell. "Come get your newspaper!" I went up and got my paper without asking any questions. I began to read every single word in that issue of the LA Times.

Soon after I sat down with my new reading material, two Mexicans came over to talk to me. The small one knelt in front of me, in a catcher's stance without his knees touching the ground. The taller one crouched behind him like an umpire, hands rested on his knees.

"My name is The Program," the small one said. He motioned behind him with a nod, "This is Danger." I nodded in understanding. "Do you know why you got a paper? Because you're white, and every group gets a paper." I nodded again.

"You're the only white boy in here, so let me tell you about The Program. You do not talk with the Blacks at all. See that half of the toilets?" he pointed. "Those are the Mexican toilets. You can use those, but only when nobody else is. Those showers," he pointed, "are the Mexican showers. You can use those, but only when nobody else is." The tables, the phones, they were all divided by race, and I could use the Mexicans', when nobody else was.

Then he said what he needed from me. "How much money do you have on your account?"

"Like twenty bucks."

"Ok you need more." He pulled a piece of paper out of his pocket and gave it to me. It was a prison commissary order form. He pulled a pencil from behind his ear and gave it to me, and told me to order candy bars for him. A lot of them. I understood; no cash, no cigarettes, so candy bars. I had to pay for my protection. Then he turned to matters of personal hygiene. Pointing at the list, directing me to the proper boxes, he told me I needed soap, razors, deodorant, etc.

He took the form from me but allowed me to keep the pencil. Then he ended – "Are you down with The Program?" He started straight through my eyes. I looked at him, then Danger, who had the same look in his eyes, then back. "Yes, sir."

"Good," and they left.

I sat on my mattress, relieved and grateful more than afraid and apprehensive. At least now I knew the rules, and knew where I stood. I went back to my paper, hoping I'd get out of there before I needed to call my girlfriend and ask her to put some money on my account.

Over the course of my time in that cell (maybe eighteen hours, time does disappear), beds became available as other left, and everyone on the floor next to me pulled up their mattresses onto a bunk, except, I realized, for me. This just made me more conspicuous, but I was unsure of what I was supposed to do exactly, and I didn't want to join them all, I was separate, I was just there because of a speeding ticket. I just wanted to be left alone. I just hoped I'd be pulled out of there soon.

At one point I did talk to someone. I was finished with my newspaper, and I saw a different one on one of the Mexicans' tables. I rose from my mattress island and sat at the table, and began to read a Spanish-language newspaper, as best as I could. I didn't care what language it was in, I just wanted something to read, so I practiced my Spanish. A worn, skinny, 30ish man with gang tattoos on his face sat next to me.

"Can you read that?" he asked.

"A little."

"What does it say?" I told him about a border skirmish between Peru and Ecuador. He looked at me stunned, but interested in what I had to say. I would not be surprised if he didn't know how to read in any language.

I never moved my mattress to a bed, and my order for The Program was never taken, as eventually enough my name was called, I was taken out of the cell, and put on another bus. Time to go back downtown, with the rumor going around we were getting released.

CONTRIBUTORS

SEAN ANDRESS's art can be found in the following places
Facebook: SeanAndressArt, Twitter: @SeanAndressArt,
Art for Sale: seanandress.etsy.com, Ebay Sales: AndressArts.

KIIK A.K. is a graduate of the University of California, Berkeley
and Santa Clara University. He earned a MA from UC Davis where
his poetics thesis was titled *THE JOY OF HUMAN SACRIFICE*
and a MFA from UC San Diego where his collection of counter-in-
ternment narratives was titled *EVERYDAY COLONIALISM*. His
work has appeared or is forthcoming in *Pleiades, The Southeast
Review, iO, Washington Square, Spork Press* and *Alice Blue Review*. The pieces included here are dedicated to poet, activist and
theorist Angela Eunsong Kim.

johnnie b. baker is the editor and publisher of Budget Press. He
has been published various places in print and online. He is cer-
tainly down with the program. budgetpress.net

ALEX BOSWORTH was born in a house he built himself in San
Diego circa 1965. His parents (no photos available) were both
teachers with theatrical backgrounds who encouraged their son to
write and read his stories before unwilling audiences from the age
of ten. Inspired by writers such as Kurt Vonnegut and Ursula K.
Le Guin, as well as monologists David Sedaris and Spalding Gray,
Bosworth reads his work at coffeehouses, bookstores and coin operated laundries throughout Southern California. His book, *Chip
Chip Chaw: Tales of the Unsane* is available online.

ROBIN WYATT DUNN writes and teaches in Los Angeles. You can
find him online at robindunn.com and Facebook.com/settdigger.

ZACHARY SCOTT HAMILTON grew up in Oregon, and spent many years traveling, where he began a fascination for the composed word. On occasion he writes for *HOUSEFIRE*. Follow him at zshuniverse.tumblr.com

RYAN HICKS is a writer and stand up comedian who regularly performs all over Southern California, mainly at all of clubs in his hometown of San Diego. He also works with local non profit organizations So Say We All and The Oldest Profession, participating in and producing a variety of literary/performance art shows like VAMP, New Best Thing, Genuine Class and Tabled. Ryan co-founded the entertainment media blog/podcast/journal *The Artificial Selection Project,* and is currently working on a comedy television pilot while finalizing the official draft of his first novel *Stupid Youth*. He enjoys spending his off time watching movies and television, listening to music and podcasts, and reading anything he can get his hands on.

BRANDON MARLON is a creative writer from Ottawa, Canada. He received his B.A. (Hon.) in Drama and English from the University of Toronto and his M.A. in English from the University of Victoria. www.brandonmarlon.com

GRANT MASON lives in Lakewood, CO. He's a construction worker and has been published in *Admit2, Nefarious Ballerina, Chopper,* and the *Rapid City Journal,* but he only likes the poem that was in *Nefarious.*

PATRICK MAYUYU is a native San Diegan. He's been seen acting, singing and dancing on several community theatre stages around town. As a writer and poet, his work has been featured in a few VAMP showcases with So Say We All, as well as with the San Diego MENding Monologues.

NEIL MCDEVITT is a non-native San Diegan, having moved from Boston a couple of years ago. He enjoys writing and performing short memoir pieces, playing golf and bragging about the nice weather outside as if it were a personal accomplishment.

CLAY NORVELL spends most of his time writing, reading, skateboarding, and playing music. He is currently working on a novella about a hardboiled P.I. in his hometown of Tulsa, Oklahoma. He can be found on Facebook or any place that serves good barbecue.

MASON GREEN RICHARDS is a senior in a creative writing class at South Eugene High School.

ALAN SEMROW lives in Wisconsin and is a graduate of English from the University of Wisconsin-Stevens Point. His poetry and fiction have been featured in multiple publications, including *BlazeVOX14, Red Fez, The Bicycle Review, Earl of Plaid Lit Journal, Danse Macabre Literary Magazine, Potluck Magazine, Blotterature Lit Mag; The Rain, Party, & Disaster Society; The Commonline Journal, Crack the Spine, Indiana Voice Journal, Former People: A Journal of Bangs and Whimpers, Golden Walkman Magazine, Barney Street*, and *Wordplay*, and he won the Essayist Award from the University of Wisconsin-Stevens Point English Department for his nonfiction work. In 2015, his stories are set to be featured in several journals, including *EAP: The Magazine, DoveTales Lit Journal*, and *The Chaffey Review*. Semrow spends the majority of his free time with his boyfriend, friends, family, and Shih Tzu, Remy.

PARKER TETTLETON is a Leo, a vegan, a resident of Portland, Oregon. He's also the author of the grocery-shopping-themed collection *Greens* (Thunderclap Press 2012) & the chapbooks *Same Opposite* (Thunderclap Press 2010) and *Ours Mine Yours* (Pity Milk Press 2014). A new collection, *August Light*, is forthcoming in 2015 from Housefire Books.

MEG TUITE's writing has appeared in numerous literary journals. She is the author of two short story collections, *Bound By Blue* (2013) Sententia Books and *Domestic Apparition* (2011) San Francisco Bay Press, and three chapbooks, the latest titled, *Her Skin is a Costume* (2013) Red Bird Chapbooks. She won the Twin Antlers Collaborative Poetry award from Artistically Declined Press for her poetry collection, *Bare Bulbs Swinging* (2014) written with

Heather Fowler and Michelle Reale. She teaches at the Santa Fe
Community College, is an editor for Santa Fe Literary Review
and Connotation Press and has a column up at *JMWW*. She lives
in Santa Fe with her husband and menagerie of pets. Her blog:
http://megtuite.com

ALLISON WHITTENBERG is a poet and author of *Life is Fine,*
Sweet Thang, Hollywood & Maine, Tutored, all from Random
House and *The Sane Asylum* from Beatdom. She lives in Philadel-
phia.

www.ingramcontent.com/pod-product-compliance
Lightning Source LLC
Chambersburg PA
CBHW072042170626
46811CB00008B/3136